# TAKE MY HAND

## Where Have I Gone

### By

### Shane Soleta

ISBN: 1-4107-4128-1 (e-book)
ISBN: 1-4107-4127-3 (Paperback)

This book is printed on acid free paper.

Cover Art: Paul Hartburg
Windom, MN

1st Books - rev. 05/22/03

# Dedication

This book is dedicated to all addicts in and out of recovery.

I would like to thank the following for inspiring and encouraging me in writing this book. To God, for saving me from myself. To my family, who never stopped loving me. To all the counselors and staff at Woodstock, with special thanks to my angel in the crow's nest. This never would have happened without you. To my home group, what could I possibly say that you have not heard, thanks for listening.

# Foreword and Introduction

Hello, my name is Shane. I am an addict. I would like to tell you a little bit about myself concerning the following poems and lyrics you are about to read. They are simply the longing of my inner most being. The pain and desperation I felt as I grew into whom I am today. Many speak of broken relationships and my anger towards authority and society as a whole. Still others are simply the crazy thoughts that swam through my head as I observed others while intoxicated with drugs.

Please note that when I mention drugs in general, I am speaking of alcohol as well. Please don't fall into the trap of thinking alcohol isn't a drug, because it is.

The story of where I came from is not nearly as important as where I am headed. I was a practicing alcoholic in my early teens, traveling the road of a progressive disease called addiction. I was twenty-six or twenty-seven the first time I stuck a needle in my arm. At thirty, I became a full blown junkie. At thirty-one death seemed welcome. Thanks to God, I checked myself into New Life Treatment Center in Woodstock, Minnesota.

I consider Woodstock my second home. This is the place where I surrendered to God all my previous beliefs and all my fears. In my early years I was a believer in God. At twenty-four I came across a system of beliefs called neo-tech. It celebrated man as the highest life form in the universe. I fell in love with the theories of power and control it offered to those who lived by its principles.

I rejected God and the Ten commandments and tried to live the neo-tech way of life. No alcohol, no drugs, no caffeine, and no sugar. If I could master these things, then I would be able to control my fellow man and thus, my future. I would amass guiltless wealth and have sex with whomever I wanted. These were the ideals of neo-tech. They also strived for biological immortality. Some of their theories are very noble and well intentioned. They lacked the most important thing, that being God. I was unable to give up the things they required and gave up on it all, but I continued to not believe in God.

The next seven years of my life were a nightmare. Drugs and alcohol became my Gods and I worshipped and sacrificed to them on a daily basis. I had a couple of brief stints of sobriety, but never serenity. I would argue with anyone who tried to tell me there was a God, and I rejected anyone who tried to reach out and help me. My alcohol and drug use grew worse and worse as well as my hatred for myself and my fellow man. I gave up on relationships and mocked any and all forms of love. When I tried to care for people in my life, I either hurt them or was hurt myself. Many of my friends took their own lives, some were murdered, some died in accidents, and others, like myself, did time in jails or prison. I hated all authority figures in my life. I blamed the government, the cops, even my own family for who I had become. It was me against the world and the world was winning.

On February 18th, 2001 I stuck a needle in my arm for the last time. Everyone in my life became demons conspiring to kill me. The many voices in my head ordered me to kill myself so that I would cause my family and friends no further shame. I debated this possibility for several hours, all the while fully expecting one of my friends to pop through the door at any minute and do me in himself. By the grace of God, I made it through that night.

The next morning my father came to the door asking my help with a project he was working on. I was a mess. I still thought people were trying to kill me, but I went with him. A few hours later I told him what I had become and that I needed help.

The twenty-first of February I checked into Woodstock. I think there were eighteen of us. The first thing I noticed was though I had never met any of these people before that day, they all seemed very familiar. It was as though I had met each and every one of them, somewhere, sometime. It was very spooky, but something within reassured me that I was exactly where I needed to be.

With the help of these newfound friends, my counselors, and the entire loving staff at Woodstock, I was able to start believing in myself again. I found God and realized he had never left my side. Even during all the years I rejected him and spoke out against his existence, he was always there. I witnessed many miracles at Woodstock. I experienced a spiritual awakening, which has forever changed my life. I formed friendships that will last forever.

Giving up alcohol and drugs left a huge void in my life. I have chosen to fill that void with God. It has not been easy. I still have cravings from time to time. Sometimes I get lonely and wonder just who I am and what my purpose. Usually, I am filled with hope and am in complete awe of all he has done for me and all my friends in recovery. As part of my program, I am striving to become a better Christian and to do unto others as I would have them do unto me.

None of this is easy. It takes constant effort on my part. Through prayer, church, and the 12 step meetings I attend, I am learning to live life on life's terms. I believe God speaks to me through my fellow addicts at these meetings. I not only struggle with alcohol and drugs, but also with lust and greed. With faith in God, through his son, Jesus Christ, I have been able to persevere. As I write this, it has been nearly twenty-four months since I last used. If you had known me before, you too,-would believe in miracles.

These poems don't even come close to describing everything I have gone through in the thirty-three and a half years of my life. They serve as constant reminders of where I have come from and where I am going. I would never expect anyone to completely understand them all. Sometimes when I read them, I'm not even sure what I was thinking or where I was coming from. Other times it seems all too clear. The frustrations and the losses experienced while using could never be accurately described with words. Neither can the joys and triumphs of living a life of recovery.

There are forty poems and lyrics written during my using days, from the time I was fifteen till the age of thirty-one. Some of these are graphic and blatantly evil. Others are filled with the anger of helplessness and loss. Some are filled with hope.

The next forty are written to those who have helped me in my recovery, to God and to all who are still struggling in recovery. Yes, I still experience dark times and times of helplessness. By reaching out to God and my friends in recovery I am able to get through them without relapsing. These poems are the most personal and filled with the most hope. For whatever reason you are reading these poems, I pray they will bring you closer to God. That you would understand he is an all forgiving God and a God who always provides and never abandons.

You will notice that several poems still question God's will for my life, and my struggle to find love without mistaking it for lust. I have seen too many people in recovery fall into this and it leads them right back to drugs. By being honest with God, I am able to get through the pain and grow even closer to him. I know the day will come when the love of my life appears. Until that day comes I will probably still struggle with temptation. It is my nature; I want everything right now.

Letting God know when I am angry at him is one of the biggest steps I have made. He already knows when I am angry, so it makes sense to tell him about it. I disagree with many things he has asked me to do. He speaks to me through my friends in recovery before, during and after meetings. I don't always like what I hear, but it is always what I need to hear.

So here it goes. If this book helps just one person find God and recovery it will be worth it. One person can influence many others in a positive way. The biggest lie I believed while using was that I was only hurting myself. I hurt friends and family more than I could ever imagine. Hopefully, by writing this book and continuing to go to meetings and working my program, God can use me to bring some hope to others. I used to cause pain. I don't want to be that way ever again. Just for today, I don't have to.

I would like to thank everyone who I have ever met, and all those who prayed for the addict who still suffers, while I was suffering, though I may never meet them. Each and every one of you has helped me become who I am today. You continue to be the inspiration that prompts me toward the spiritual path of recovery, giving me a better understanding of God and his plan for me.

May God Bless You Always, shane

# A Letter to the Stars

I went down to the park with
a pain in my heart.
I stared at the sky and I wondered,
What response would I get,
or am I crazier yet,
If I wrote a letter to the stars.

Would the seven sisters weep,
if I told them my grief?
Would Polaris write back,
or would he just laugh
at the scribbling of me,
a minute-creature?
I'm alone here on earth
with nothing of worth,
my words and my dreams
they mean nothing.

I've been cast from the norms
of the slaves and the swarms
and I thank God he gave me that much.

For I will not believe
there is nothing to do.
Is the answer in the sky?
If so, tell me why.
Why cannot somebody see?
Why can't someone be?
Why won't the stars answer me?

# Awaken

Behind the bridge of eyes, deceive
Wizard's word shall follow thee
Listen to the mind when blind
Pain a treasure, you will find
Cherish what the heart reveals
You'll never keep, what you must steal
Pearly eyes drip blood and wine
Cheat yourself, you can't cheat time
If your search finds honesty
You'll never have to dream you're free

Through it all, when battle torn
There is an end, to every storm
If you let it, time will heal
Never be afraid to feel
Live and learn, will cleanse the soul
Someday find, your dream to hold.

# Beyond an Endless Night

Our hands embrace the falls
a smile and a kiss
Lips like rosy petals
an arrow shot from Heaven
One that did not miss

A river standing still
A night that should not end
Soft kiss to the cheek
Our hearts create the beat
of feelings kept within

Tell me all your secrets
I'll show you my favorite star
Northern lights are breathing
Night owl whispering
Fucking with our hearts

The tears I almost cried
They are yet to come,
I can see the future
before it shows its face
We may never have one.

But for now we laugh
Play the game of dreams
We'll search and then pretend
Find the rainbow's end
This we must believe.

*Shane Soleta*

# Birds Will Fly

Sunrise falling sky
Beyond the clouds she hides
Beauty fast asleep
Distant star, drifting free
Feeling hazy purple
Color of all my dreams
Life behind the scenes
Battle of wise men and fools
My head and heart as tools
Weapons of the soul
Thoughts I never told
River running pain
Constant it remains
Each and every change

Yes, I dream of beauty
Still I fear her eyes
For if I hold her heart
Someday I'll make her cry
She will persecute me
Ravage my excuse
Destroy me with her words
Kill me with her hurt
All of this I know
No longer wonder why
Just the way it is
Just like birds will fly.

# Come Now Dance with Me

I feel it overwhelming, now each day it grows
Days will turn to hours, minutes drawing close
When my blues seal shut, I'll hear the golden words
I'll visit my friends' dreams, whisper through the birds
May they be at peace, with my memories
I'll rest in someone's heart, until she sets me free
No one bares the fault, of what they did to me
For I knew all along, better no one believed
It was just a vision, a feeling I only knew
Now I'm no longer empty, I'm full just like the moon
I tried to do my best, but I always wanted more
I was warned of this, when I unlocked the door
Always I've been sick, always I have failed
But with defeat is victory, now my ship has sailed
With each storm I conquered, another came behind
But I always lead the way, searching just to find
Put roses on my grave, exchange them for my dreams
May they come true for you, some day then you'll see
The picture I have drawn, it was meant for you
True love lives at sunset, just like we used to
Do not cry for me, tears are just in vain
Never change a thing, just bring back the pain
Motionless I lay, with smile on my face
Finally I'm content, or was I just a waste.

*Shane Soleta*

# Buried Treasure

Scavengers of heart light
Let the savage scream
Bloody midnight darkness
Beckoning to me

Lift your vultures higher
Release them to the trees
The hives of hell spill out
Capture fast the queen

Arrow of betrayal
Sticking out my heart
Squealing pig impaled
These are not the stars

Two warriors rot and stink
Planting life and death
Lie and laugh away
Dragons never slain

Shadows of the kingdom
Graves of love and war
Forever in the ground
Two dreams never found.

# Dead Pool

Laying down in a pool.
Water warm as blood.
At the bottom of a hillside
I tread through the pain of the dead,
I notice printed rocks-
poems of a lost century
writers unknown, as voices unheard
for six feet of earth, silences
that yearn for recognition.

My dreams are alive
in the faces, of those
whose dreams have died.
My eyes climb the slope, of
dry, withered grass,
rotting trees, those stones
which broke away, from
the once tidy fort on top.
Misery, grabs at me to follow,
but I will not.
No sadness, no tears
for what many fear, I swim
through their cries
well into night.

*Shane Soleta*

The sky is filled
with millions of wishes,
I think I might want to claim one.
I look to the moonlight,
absorbed in the rocks, and wish,
never to be one.

# Flee

I sat next to God
and laughed at the fools.
I sat there in hell
and laughed at their rules.

My turn with fire
My hand in hell
Escape not for you
Shall join me as well

I light up my cancer
Inhale my doom
Tears of the angels
My father the moon

Darkness my child
The eyes of the stars
They watch over all
My sky full of scars

Invading our souls
Disposing our dreams
The waste of our minds
From the earth flee.

*Shane Soleta*

# Hail all Leaders

The witch confessed
Blue boys blessed
White-laced dream
will meet its death.

No warning shot
The door explodes
Come legal evils
who sold their souls.

With silver fire
Turned back shots
Children cry
As lives are dropped

Headline hit list
Blue boys proud
How many dreams
They shot down

Educated
Schools of sin
Paid to hate
Who doesn't fit in

Hypocrite freedom
Rule by fear
Money made smiles
Been stealing for years

Elected parasites
On sickness they prey
Silence their victims
Locked in a cage.

*Shane Soleta*

# Life

From ever over the mountain
The wind sings life in my ears
Waves through my body, it dances
I sway to the music like
a tree in the wind
Gentle motion I move to
make love to the night
I kiss nature's breast
Under moonlight, I confess
The yearn from within
The mouth of a river
A pressure as violent as
a storm fast approaching
Now, is the moment of pain
Let the sky bleed as I
Let the sun die, as
My love in her eyes
Let my maker feel as I.

# Dead Spot Dance

Shot into a star
A falling, spreading glare
The lady branded wisdom
Wears loose her silver hair

Darkness on the throne
A jewel turned to stone
Dead dance escape the night
Let go the coward's life

A decorated princess
Painted royal red
Keep her soul on level
A prince she'll surely wed

Veil of rosebud honey
She wears around her heart
Enough is never plenty
Take now back you are

Wait for you till danger
Warnings printed loud
Hid behind my blush
A dead spot in the crowd

*Shane Soleta*

# Gold Creates

Black eyes beneath the night
Blood dripping candle light
My heart is set aflame
Pleasure, torture, shame

When wild eyes agree
They put me on my knees
Backstab through the heart
Another waits to start

Inside, when it rains
I stare a sunny day
Drift away from pain
Fade into a haze

My skies are always changing
Just like day and night
Confusion is remaining
Never get it right

When I see a rainbow
I am nearly there
It disappears in Heaven
and the gold creates a fool

# Image Head

I count the fading faces
Twenty-one sky blue
Turning point now clear
Black roses in full bloom

Where fire burns the icy cold
Heaven falls in tears
Above the timberline ascends
The spirit's wind I fear

The crackling branches sing
Too familiar tale
No use defending dreams
With fast approaching hell

Who dares to creep within
Theses visions of the night
Moving painted things
Closed eyes black and white

Night will take a picture
Freeze frame without chase
Gather at the bonfire
Wither in its face

*Shane Soleta*

# Maker of Me

River colossus, reflecting the green
Guardians of time, endless supreme
Down on my knees
Sip life from the stream
Nourishing river
The maker of me

Comfort me mother
My head under water
Choking on you
The maker of me

Push me down under
Open your eyes
Let me taste freedom
Spit up your lies

They drown me in sorrow
Bring guilt to my mind
No reason regrets
I have my own life
The dreamer is doing
A stroke at a time
No longer dependent
Goodbye changing tides

Rising, receding
Forever I'm blind
Now I'm uplifting
Now I am mine

16

# Goodbye my love

Lavender and crystal blue
Background music
to enhance you,
Secrets revealed,
your broken heart is bleeding

To love is to kill
I cut you wide open
pray that your wounds are not fatal

I feel your pain
Though you don't know
to forgive is to hate
and I can't blame you

Thinking I loved you so true
So messed up inside
I only hurt you

Held each other tight
Oh, so many times
Love overwhelmed us
Devoured us blind
Never again,
Is what I say now
It will happen again
Always does somehow

*Shane Soleta*

Can't tell you lies,
Then kiss you goodbye
Lied to myself
and your loving eyes

I could have tried
To make it work
Girl, you know
Would only make it hurt worse

Love may remain
in the feelings we hide
We grow apart
in time we divide
Our cross has been planted,
Goodbye!

# Liquid Shadow

*Shane*

A cross-eyed crooked hand
Extending touch to you
Liquid eyes cool blue
Following,
Seeking out your truth,
The moon brings life
to shadows
The trees sing rhymes
of gloom. The scarecrow
blown away. Dark face,
cold content. The night
is where it crept
Open,
Empty grave,
The shadow found its way
Liquid eyes cool blue
A presence in your room
Feelings run and hide
The seer spoke too soon
Trembling,
Sweating skin,
A picture sinking in
The truth will let you live
The shadow comes to take
Extend your touch and give.

# Open Eyes Die

The light still beckons
I still decline
Searching for truth
I can not find
Why does she rule my mind?

A taste of danger
Twelve red roses burning
My heart a twisted wire
Circles fly, my head is turning
Nothing there, and she's still burning.

The dream, it will not happen
When the time is right
Dissection while alive
Pain which crucifies
Open eyes, and dreams will die.

Blew you out, then lit you up
And blew you out again
Your fire lit up paradise,
But I'm too scared to smile
The tears inside I hide
Another night,
When my heart cries
The dream, it will not die.

# Naked Nature's Heart

Taste the passion dripping sweet
Mouthwatering from the springs of heat
Bathe in tear-filled, wishful eyes
Young girl's hope, betrayed by lies

A love which breathed in star-blue skies
Hot breath burning like sunshine
Rainbows come and she found gold
Cast a fire, dragons scold

Secrets which she never tells
Framed in pictures, hang in hell
Wicked one who freed her sin
The jackal laughs, a two faced grin

White cloud once an angel's heart
Black night conquers, then departs
With naked nature, desire yearned
Innocent forest eyes have burned

Young seed blossoms, womanhood
Misguided love, misunderstood
Cherry sweet, with bitter dreams
Runaway tears, her blood red sea

*Shane Soleta*

# Mystery

Turning round
To follow you
The darkest eyes
I see through
Mystery,
Your love I need
Come back now
I beg, you tease
Mystery,
Before I scream
Slap my face
and shake this dream
If I could
I'd show you love
But long ago
My heart gave up

The twisted nights
Where I live
Dare not ask
You to come with

One small smile
I'm in a rage
Please let me be
I can't change

Holding hands
I picture this
Oh my God
To taste your kiss

Touching you
Trembling
Loving you
This cannot be

Close my eyes
But I can't hide
Still you breathe
Deep in my mind

*Shane Soleta*

# My Love

Sense the approaching blindness
Arrow off the mark
The feelings you fought so hard for
Burn away, as you fall apart

Lightning razorblades
Cutting through your veins
My God, my God, the pain
Standing in the flames

Love bleeds from your eyes
Everyday and night
Books you studied hard
Put you right back at the start

They say live and learn
I say love and let it burn
For if it did not hurt
It was never really earned.

# Living Sacrifice

Love within you
Where does it hide?
Eyes of angels
Why do they lie?

Skin touch satin
How does it breathe?
Scarlet letters
Worn on your sleeve

Shoot me in your vein
Maybe I can help
Which way to your heart
When you're blown away

Want to look into the skies
Where your eyes have been
Want to know just how it feels
To be alive yet dead

*Shane Soleta*

# Nowhere

Sometimes when I dream
I sit back and I scream
Wonder why it's me
Who loses everything

I try to please the world
It just shits on me
I try to please a girl
She just wants to leave

I plant a bed of roses
So I can watch them die
Never find the answer
Asking myself why

An oasis in the desert
Is what they promised me
I am just a vagrant
As far as they can see

I reach within for strength
I vomit and I plead
The race for life is lost
Crying on my knees

I'm cut down to the roots
I've given up on prayer
My life, it seems, it sucks
For me there is nowhere.

# Meth

Scatterbrain
Electric fear
The time has come
My stars are near

Whisper-moon
Shadow-hawk
Scare beyond
Where creatures stalk

Lost of Heaven
Bitter wind blows
Five o'clock night
Who cast the first stone

Wings which fly
Oceans ahead
Watch us all die
Come bury the dead

*Shane Soleta*

# Measure the Distance

The devil's hiss
A certain smile
Starlight kiss
Hold my breath
A fire burns
The distance
A fire burns
Bleed
Fire melting flesh
Red hot sweating skin
Survivor howls
Once again
The distance
Song of the owl
Lubricate
The vulgar tongue
Fire burns
The distance
Once again
The vulgar tongue

# As I Descend

Now as I descend
On this road to nowhere
Try hard as I can
Still I wonder when

Voices are repeating
Same as yesterday
Alone, the tone did change
Still it hurts the same

Simply said, I dream
Loudly, I report
Quietly, I hide
The target, I don't seek

Tear away my wings
Don't want to fly in sorrow
The crown of kings does beckon
I cringe and do not follow

Shame, the price I claim
My soul will not dissent
Parts of me are gone
Show me where they went

Lost is not a word
Which describes me justly
I'm blown away by life
Yet, too afraid to die

*Shane Soleta*

Someone please do tell me
Take my hand and show me
Give my eyes the truth
Help me find what's gone

# Waco

I watched the children
runaway,
and seen there bodies
burning in the day.
Flowers bloomed from them
and exploded into the heads of demons.

Trumpets blared from the amber
rays of the setting sun.
Away in flames
a million dreams
a thousand lives never seen
ashes behind
can't hide the pain.

They never agree and
the dead seldom speak.
So how do I believe?
When we kill our own,
then grieve…

Anger numb trance
through smoke and the screams.
How dare we dance
and murder the meek…

*Shane Soleta*

# Searching for Myself

Lost within my self-perception
Acid is my rain
Myriad of tears
My cloud-drenched clothing clinging
To the hope, of something, unclear

From this windy shelter
Fading pictures in my mind
I pray to God for guidance
And reject his comfort blind

My travel agents, wings
Those who sing at morning's light
Enchant my soul, curse me with dreams
I embrace their vision
But fail at flight

Search for gold with double vision
Ponder which door to open
My brothers and sisters, another dialect,
A code which can't be broken

All life's mysteries remain
Mathematics is not life
All answers are repeating
Then changing like the tides

As a child of the moon
My dark side never seen
Not even eagles' eyes may pry
Into my deep black sea

So I sit, and shake, and tremble
My cold heart, froze within
I'm a skipping stone, on water
Stop!
Now I'm sinking in

*Shane Soleta*

# Seeing Ghosts

Gathered round the water green,
golden ghosts I think I've seen.
Danced with death throughout the night
beneath the flames which show no light.

Futile grasp of yesterday,
let go my neck and evil ways.
Trampled neathe a fiery fate
by my own storm which I create.

Lightning strikes, a million times
when we choose, to be blind.
How far above the clouds are they
who could not heal the pain they saved.

Do they live, even when they die?
How many tears have wondered why?
If the question is, just who we are.
We must decide then just how far.

Push away till we're out of reach.
How can we learn if we do not teach?
Golden ghosts will never help
when we feed the fire and burn ourselves.

# Nights we Deny

The twenty-ninth time, they laid out a line
I turned my head, to deny

There she was, standing in the corner
With the eyes of a gun, and the smile of a blade

She said,
You better have fun, because,
Sooner or later
You better run,
And you better take me

Nights we deny, hot like the fire
The fire which burns, inside my veins

Nights we deny, we get higher and higher
Higher and higher, so high and so free

My shadow an angel, yet I run with the devil
Why can't I get it, straight in my head

I know the answers, to all of your questions
But I can't remember, a thing that I did

The demons within
The best of my friends
How many times
Must I witness death?
Before I decide I want to live!

*Shane Soleta*

# Silent Thoughts

Hands which refused to pray
shaking fast with rage.
The God I did forsake
has claimed another today.

Preacher's words will fade,
same way as my faith.
In time, perhaps the pain,
echoing through my veins.

Sky has turned to gray.
Tears spit out like venom.
Cruel is the wind,
slaps my bitter face.

Why, the looming question
Fear is welcomed in.
If it can happen once
Surely it will again.

This we all must live through
never knowing a thing.
How much must we suffer
before they crown are king?

# Slipping

Three dead roses,
crystal vase,
the kitchen table, where you
left notes for your mother.

I stop to take a look,
two red, one pink,
soon brown.
I know its not there yet,
but you await below the steps.

The road to your heart
is puzzles and rhymes.
A mountain too high
and jagged to climb.

I know cuz I fell
now my heart burns in hell.
My dreams turn to nightmares
with your absence.
Yet, closer to you
brings my heart closer to death.

Hanging from a cliff,
holding only fear.
Grab my hand
and hold it tight.
But you can't lift me up.
Still you hold on tight,
Slipping.

*Shane Soleta*

# Silence

Silence,
Kills the guilty
Makes them think
When evil thoughts
So often speak

Voices of the wind, usually go unheard
on this silent night, you hear unspoken words.

Messages they send, excite your wild sense.
Smoke a wicked number, before you get too tense.

Relax and soak it in, skin will start to crawl.
Held back for awhile, till again the voices call.

Raised up from your rest, slowly start to move
Controlled by the unseen, one on one with you

Deep into the darkness, following the sound
Grip unwanted desires, strange feelings abound

Think you may be lost, nothing you can see
Take to the right trail, hold true to your instincts

Finally see the light, reached your wicked goal
Now everything is blank, now you lost your soul

Wake up knowing nothing, feeling just like hell
Walls surround you now, wake up in a cell.

# Stop

From round the world
gather the breed.
Where life everlasting
is challenged with greed.

Fly down from Heaven
this vast state of mind.
Tell them about freedom
The lies which they hide.

Holy their haven
Dare you embrace
Beware of the demons
behind smiling face.

Truth is an abstract
of what you believe.
How to be honest,
without being guilty.

Say what you will
you shall be free.
Great dragon slayer
punishing thee.

The answer is cancer
dwells far within.
You cannot fight
what you cannot rid.

*Shane Soleta*

Let go your poisons
trample and stab.
Flee the enigma
before it grabs back.

For without its host
Its power is gone.
Let loose its life
and yours shall live on.

# Stranger in the Twilight

I sense the presence of an enemy
as I sit alone at night.
My dying wish, one last kiss
from the killer who grips the knife.

For it is she, whom I have known,
for many of my years.
And as her eyes, watch my back
I tremble,
yet without fear.

For I know, and always will
cuz it's always been so near.
Now I see the end draw close
I'm crying,
yet without tears.

For me there is no tomorrow
yet why should that bring sorrow.
The stranger things are yet to come
and come they will, you'll see.
For the emptiness,
which I possess,
has always been killing me.

*Shane Soleta*

# The Core of all Danger is One's Own Mind

The exotic symptom
has been planted
in the memory of mankind.

They kill at will
to fulfill
the passion which leads them blind.

Through each other and eternity
to all the depths of hell,
the mind is too blind to see.

If ever a soul
was released from blindness,
what then comes of thee.

For it is unlikely
with such power
that there is control.

Yet the only answer
is hidden well
and never will be known.

# Take My Hand

If in pain
come take my hand.
Not forever
but now and then.

I can't commit
to one soul now.
For mine's still lost
out there alone.

In the clouds
I've caught rainbows.
In the sand
I've struck gold.

But in the eyes
when I gave love.
I seen them cry
cuz I gave up.

I bled secrets
and opened wounds.
Betrayed the trust
which I consumed.

So don't look up
for I'm not there.
I'm just a thought
who tried to care.

*Shane Soleta*

Be my friend
and let me go.
Take my hand
come back my soul.

# Unwritten Penetration

Unwritten penetration
Shadows of my voice
I scream into the hearts
of those without rejoice.
The unknown feels so real
Give to you my fear
Return to me your own
The lost will know my name

For I am of the breed
Different ways we see
Our Heaven scattered starlight
Hell is what we feel

Search through me your thoughts
A night you cannot sleep
A dream refuse, remember
If ever you awake

Like before I'm you
Those who watch the world
Eyes descending blue
Home without a place
Lost without a face
Turning into dust

*Shane Soleta*

# They Can't Wait to See

All angels in the sky
Come kiss this night goodbye
My moon is never full
My stars just fade away

A witness to the end
An everlasting sin
Fatal is the joy
Only love destroys

My heart is like the tree
that has lost its leaves
It fights against the wind
Cracking, caving in

Songbirds fly away
Scavengers perch and wait
They want to be my friend
They want to see my end

Bring your gasoline
They can't wait to see
Pour it over me
They know I'll light the fire.

## Will Not Die

Put your arms around me.
Do you feel what I feel?
If you don't shake
and you don't fall,
then I know you ain't real.

Don't tell me you've been there
don't lie and pretend.
Your twelve steps through hell
don't compare, where I've been.

Fly away angels
till the blue turns to gray.
Go somewhere and cry
for a life, who won't be saved.

Many, many, years
listened to advice.
These twisted laws of hate
are wrong and they are right.

How could anyone
who thinks for themselves?
Believe in all the lies
that our government sells.

*Shane Soleta*

Guess how many now,
locked up in cage.
How many prison cells,
hold secrets, we need
that we may be saved.

Label them crazy fools
But they know, oh yes they do.
That's why they will not listen,
to the likes of you.

The masses all lay down, when Uncle Simon says.
How sad that it must be, to simply just exist.

It throbs and yes, it screams, at least I feel alive.
No matter when they say I'm gone, I'm here, I will not die!

# Where Goes the Dim Blue light

Where goes the dim blue light
Enveloped in blackness
Through the veins of innocence
Travel down the right
Muddled red
Purple haze approaching
Up the left
Against gravity
Against reason
Why!
The shock of harmful things
Desire of dark delight
Bliss of anti-life
Black out the ghost of Christ
Head on hit
Heart which screams
Laughter cries
Inside a mind
that wants to die.
Where goes the dim blue light?

And

Then

I

Found

God

# A love like Yours

Though we depart – this morning of the Lord
Let us find our faith – God's love and his support

Brothers and sisters – husband and wife
As children of God – we experience life

This test of love – He gives to all
The test of resistance – when distance calls

Strengthen our hearts – so tears may flow free
When the healing starts – then we learn to see

Directions we face – our opposite poles
Dreams which we chase – let them be known

His love still abounds – may we not be blind
Stars in the sky – are the stars in your eyes

May they remind us – whenever we pray
Soon you'll be together — in the land of lakes

It will be known – if you let it be shared
A love like yours – never ends in despair.

*Shane Soleta*

# Ask the Lord

Let it rain
and let it pour
Set free the pain
and brave the storm

Life is love
and God is life
Live it well
all day and night

We have the keys
Let go the chains
Set free your will
Let God today

For all its worth
it is worthwhile
Behind the tears
the soul does smile

The Lord will know
when you let go
With his love
you have control

Do not ask me
what to do
Ask the Lord
he loves you too.

# Bedtime

Sky of Angels
Heaven above
Purge my demons
This night of love

The brightest light
that guides us home
Shines full this night
I'm not alone

My Lord, my love
My voice of faith
I pray to you
Show me the way

Cast out demons
Tormenting foes
Strike them down
With all my hope

Forgive my sins
And let me live
Show mercy to those
Who would drag me in

I need you Lord
And want to serve
These demons of mine
I beg, you'll purge

*Shane Soleta*

Let the moon shine
Full of love
Open my heart
To the stars above

My Lord, my love
I beg you please
Allow me peace
So I may sleep.

# Backseat Driver

Do I hear you calling me?
Do you want me to come now?
Do your angels follow me?
Whispering without sound.

You know that I have fallen Lord
and I have let you down.
My guard has fallen with my lust
the demons gather round.

I pray you will forgive me Lord
you know I want to do right.
But I give into the evil one
pretend I am in flight.

Miracles which I have seen
How would I not believe?
Please Lord I beg for mercy
Please help my unbelief.

Still I worry and I fear
This means I still have doubts
and I'm not doing everything
to honor you in and out.

Please Lord fill my heart
Please Lord open my eyes
I give to you my fears
I'm ready to let you drive.

*Shane Soleta*

# Believe it and try

I think of Waco
I want to cry
What you've done for me
I won't deny

You always listened
With ears from above
I listened too
Don't give up

You know what he needs
Believe in his love
Let God do the work
With the love of his Son

Live by your prayers
and give her a chance
You have been forgiven
Let time understand

We've all been hurt
We've all been scared
Love from the heart
Live by the word

Eyes which can cry
Have lived enough lies
Love defeats pride
Believe it and try.

# Blessed are the Fears

All I know is what he is
All I am is the love he gives
He is with me all the time
I used to run and I used to hide

The tears I cry are the things I do
I hurt so many and forgave so few
Lord , your love it makes me high
All I did was open my eyes

Thank you now for all you are
You lift me up so I don't fall far
I cursed your name and you were there
I despised your love and you still cared

I am dust, you are the sky
Evil blows me in your eyes
Rain pours down and now I grow
With your tears you bless my soul

Blessed are the tears
I know you cry for me
Blessed are the fears
that brought me close to thee.

*Shane Soleta*

# Courage

Secrets will betray you.
Secrets from which you scare.
Don't let them be your ruin.
Don't let them keep you here.

Secrets in the wind
blow throughout the earth.
What you think you hide,
your eyes still show the world.

Mountains start to grow
with each passing lie.
Dreams will suffocate
when you choose to hide.

Nothing is for free
Negotiating mind
Sorrow stakes a claim
when you give into thee.

The soul belongs to love.
Let go the ego beast.
The earth guide only dwells
in hearts which hide their face.

Open up to God
and all of those you love.
Secrets spoke out loud
are secrets long deceased.

# Dare I Demand

Come now my Lord
I'm calling you
I need a sign
What shall I do?

The day grows close
I'm going home
My shield is up
My love is found

Out there again
My friends, amends
Will they accept
The way I am

I love them all
Just as you
I fear them still
As I fear you

I want to be
That glorious child
Who makes you proud
Who makes you smile

I don't want this
I don't want that
You know what I need
You know where I'm at.

*Shane Soleta*

# Don't Want to Run

My lord, my Love
My love of all loves
From here on earth
to the Heavens above
May my cries for help
not go unheard
May all my fears
calm with your word
I know you're here
I know you're there
Still at times
I feel so scared
Oh Lord, My God
I beg of you
For strength
For courage
For faith as true
As true as your love
Bright like the sun
Please show me the way
Too tired to run
I just want to live
I just want to love
Just want to feel safe
and I don't want to run.

# Feeling God

I'm feeling like
alive tonight.
This night I praise
the God of light.

The God of love
Same as thine
Heals my soul
and I fly.

He's touched my heart
and set me free.
No longer bound
by selfish dreams.

I'm letting go
and letting God.
I'm turning up
not shutting down.

I'm thanking him
who lives within.
Who holds me close
forgives my sins.

Thank you God
For this night
For this love
For this life.

*Shane Soleta*

# God's Way

I will never forget that day
Just the words we said
we can laugh and that's o.k.
you helped me to want to live.

When I think of you
Bright lights in the sky
Ozzy and the rain
Mikey and all our pain

Woodstock has been blessed
May God blow you a kiss
With you he has worked wonders
Share it with the rest

Always speak your mind
Don't forget your heart
God created you
You are a work of art

Praise him and let go
He'll take away your pain
Many have been touched
He speaks through you each day

Sometimes Tonya's way
May lead you astray
Fold your hands and pray
God makes no mistakes.

# Everyday

I waited for life
to breathe with the truth.
Waited for God
to signal and call.
Waiting for myself
to open up and see
the splendor of God
through the trees with the breeze.

Seven falls down
The anxious await
Yet I dare to fear
What might my fate
All the way up, I whistled to me
How awesome it is
I can still see

Yet my eyes are like
Wind Mountain Cave
Push myself along
and I pay and I pay
and the beauty of life, I catch a glimpse
What would they think
if I stumbled and tripped.

Life extends its hand
I touch it and pray
Let all of it in
like this was my last day.

*Shane Soleta*

# Mother

The seventh of eight
late afternoon.
One hundred and two
boom, boom, boom.

One thing, then another
it all goes wrong.
But my thoughts are with mother
and a comforting song.

God please be with her
A blossoming peace
Allow her to heal
All pain be released

Her prayers have saved me
when I wandered in pain.
I mocked her love of you
she never gave way.

She honored your name
and loved me the same.
Blessed are you both
I'm alive thanks to grace.

# From God, with Love

Remember now I love you
and I always will.
Since your mother's womb
I am with you still.

You are like the stars
lighting up the dark.
All I need to know
feel it in your heart.

Each day the sun does rise
think of me and smile.
Know that you are loved
and have been all the while.

Even when there's pain
The Heavens open up
Tears will fall like rain
and wash it all away.

You may have your doubts
be patient when you pray.
A soul that wants to heal
grows stronger with your faith.

Open up your heart
Let all of my love in
It's really up to you
to let your life begin.

*Shane Soleta*

# How I Became

I tell you now – not what there is
I've known that place – called emptiness

I felt the knives – cut deep inside
My guts bled acid – out my eyes

Behind the wheel – my mind was lost
Sipping venom – till I was tossed

Into the world – of neverland
Where many go – at dark command

I followed suit – and did not know
What I dared – was my own soul

I danced in fire – and cast out spells
Each hit I took – I challenged hell

Suddenly – there was no room
For what was good – and what I knew

I wanted more – I wanted death
So I lit up – and held my breath

I gasped for air – my guts, my pain
It all spilled out – sweat like rain

Just one shot – just one time
Let loose my soul – let go my mind

Somehow years – passed me by
And my whole life – became them times

I thank you lord – who spared my life
I praise you Lord – now I'm alive

*Shane Soleta*

# I Am

A fortnight through November
Sun still shining bright
Sixty-five and still alive
Winter delays it bite

My rear end on the sidewalk
My back against the bricks
Breathe in Indian Summer
The warmth becomes my fix

God's plan I do accept
No demons I crave today
All I need is here with me
God's love is on display

Blue skies with shades of white
Has made my spirit right
There is no other place
I'd rather be right now

The years I ran away
Have settled back on me
I think I understand
I am just who I am

No need be judging others
To see where I fit in
All of us God's children
I am just who I am

I give and I have taken
Tried to place the blame
I am just who I am God
At least you never change

*Shane Soleta*

# Let Go

Empty thoughts
May overflow
Run out my mouth
Toward wanton foe

I fight these things
and pray their gone
I take them back
and linger on.

Punish my mind
Wound my soul
Don't want to forgive
Myself, though I know

I lay awake
and ponder these
I won't give in
I must release

Open up
and let me in
The doors to Heaven
I want to live

I want a taste
Not ready to go
Will she find me soon
Before I let go.

# Let your Dreams See

The spirit is with you
a priceless guide.
Now let him lead
and clear out your eyes.

The demons behind you
can not escape.
The wrath of our God
you just have to pray.

Your family awaits you
dreams are set free.
The love of your daughter
has been redeemed.

I'll say a prayer,
you say one too.
Remember your savior
who died for you.

Love everyone
as you do the Lord.
No one can hurt you
throw doubt out the door.

Remember Woodstock
Realize the dream
Love is eternal
Let your heart see.

*Shane Soleta*

# Our Angel of Hope

When you smile
Angels sing
When you laugh
We see your dreams

Even when we cry
We are being selfish
We will not say goodbye
Your presence we will miss

We love you like a mother
We trust you with our fears
In you we see an angel
We trust you with our tears

The Lord is working through you
We understand his ways
We pray that God may bless you
And we can do the same

We are not alone
You have taught us well
God is always with us
For his love we fell

Thank you for his message
Thanks for all his love
To some it is the crow's nest
We know you're a dove.

# Power of Dictation

The politics of love
God is teaching you
Humility alone
It may pull you through

Take no step for granted
Power will take hold
By humbling yourself
You've already grown

Prayer works through faith
In yourself you must believe
By asking God for help
Qualified to receive

Dare not take the credit
It's written in the word
Be honest with your fears
Understand the hurt

Sometimes with his strength
We forget from whom it came
Nothing gets done alone
Remember what you know

Give thanks and always pray
Live it day by day
God has all the knowledge
We can just dictate

*Shane Soleta*

# No Matter What

My mind projects
repeating pain
and I reject
the will to pray.

My life recedes
and then it climbs.
Seems I'm wrecked
and out of time.

Old man, young man,
who survives?
Slipping, sliding,
the choice is mine.

I get one call.
Who will it be?
Life or death
to comfort me.

Death is easy
it's all I know.
Life is hard
don't let me go.

I want to be
the wind and rain.
I want to fly
on eagle's wings.

# Spread Your Wings

May this day
eclipse the life
from hence you came
from hence you died.

May this night
embrace your love
from those still here
from those above.

You are only as sick
as the secrets reveal.
To the mind who lies
to the mind who steals.

Keep coming back
and the gift we share.
Will always be yours
we will always care.

Shout out the cliché
one day at a time.
Adds up to a year
adds up to a life.

The N.A. way
is the way to life.
Let go and let God
spread your wings and fly.

*Shane Soleta*

# Surrender Myself to Thee

From Holy waters
I breathe in dreams
The serpent dies
in blinding white.

I watched his eyes
fade into gray.
Now my souls
will revelate.

Longer now
away the pain.
All is done
with hope and faith.

I surrender myself
this very day
and watch the white
where spirits play.

They dance in threes
and show me these
for now again
we are set free.

By grace of God
I'm witnessing
Today we win
and Abba's pleased.

# This Love

The falls I've seen – have washed away dreams
My dreams I pray,
Reverberate.
Listen to me, before I scream
before it seems
it is too late.
This life of mine – falls down with pride
of those times
ruled by eyes
of the night.
I loved those lies
my nasty tongue – prodigal son
is he, who, I – who next may cry
out of these lungs
out of these tries
so futile are they – who think they create.
My only God – my only love
without him, without his Son.
I would cease – my heart would die
My love of me – my love of life.

So I open up, and pray to thee
who rules all those – who claim to be
the special one
my special love.
My God, my Lord, who gave his Son
He gives to me
this life
this love.

*Shane Soleta*

# Human Nature

Sometimes I…,
Sink into the depths,
pretend I do not care,
what may happen next.

Sleep throughout the day
welcome back the pain.
Feels like I am home
when I am alone.

My love, I serenade
beyond the deepest dreams.
Her face I cannot see
she hides away from me.

I shut the angels out
let the demons in.
Desire fills my heart
I revel in my sin.

When I do let go,
emptiness sets in.
Plead with God for mercy
forgiveness for my sins.

I know before the fact – and do it anyway
Sometimes I choose to fight – sometimes I take the bait

Pray to God for help – reject it anyway
Choose to let him in – just to sin again

I pray and pray and pray
I sin and sin and sin
Thank God for you Jesus
You are my only way in.

*Shane Soleta*

# Gone away

Gone away the wind
Laughter echoing pines
Forest burns within
Controlling life a lie

Old Gods gone away
Now I miss the pain
Night went on for days
Did not care to die

Rage in isolation
Rewarding my self-will
Scary, scary dreams
Ones I used to live

Eyes the wilderness
Serenade the depths
Soul refuse to tame
New God hear me pray

Your promises I think
Still I am unsure
What you ask of me
Feeling not so free.

# Hole

Wind it seems
Take my dreams
Rain on distant seas

Knees on ground
Pray their found
God are you around

Wear my faith
Sing your praise
Run, run, run away

Need repair
My despair
Cannot hide nowhere

My disease
Love I need
Why you let me leave

You would know
Where my soul
Come now fill this hole.

*Shane Soleta*

# Where Have I Gone

Broken dreams
Run down this mountain
Where hope has bled
And been sun baked

I try to squeeze
a little faith
fragile taste
blows away

Granite cliffs
Steeple pines
Reminding me
What's left behind

Chiseled stones
Photographs
Memories
Fade to black

Take it back
Can't hold on
Those times are gone
We were wrong

Still don't cry
Still don't try
Any thing
Any dream

Here I lay
Wooden bridge
Mountain high
And all of this

Seems too much
My insides
Twist and fight
With my mind

I thought I knew
And had enough
My life was planned
Call my bluff
I've not a clue
Where I go
Where I am
Who is I

Eight months clean
Still my life
Lost again
I can't find

Pray to God
Help me see
Close my heart
Scared of thee

Of what he asks
Don't think I can
My ego beats
My heart again

83

*Shane Soleta*

I dwell in pain
I like it there
Feels like home
Just like back there

My scrambled brain
Blacks out the norms
Of those who dared
To show they cared
I blasted them
Behind their back
With eyes of death
I walked the track

Where few do go
And then return
I've tried, I've tried
Now I burn

Desire kills
And I am full
Want so bad
To fill that hole
Evil thoughts
Provoke my needs
They have changed
again today

I wanted God
Yet I crave pain
I want to love
But can I wait

Help me God
I'll try to try
To let you in
Before I die.

*Shane Soleta*

# Where Was I

Falling through the holes
With those who lived like ghosts
Gathered in the taverns
Spears shoot out their mouths

My wounds bled in secret
I did not even know
Seemed I just felt different
Surely, I didn't care

Clueless, I soon joined them
Shooting, smoking, drinking
We planned our suicides
And did not even know

Our guilt turned into laughter
For those who let it show
We ostracized and demonized
Gladly gave our souls

There must have been a reason
We refused to fly
We played our childish games
Pretended every night

Some of us have died
Some of us still try
By the grace of God
I am still alive

# I Will Not Sway

When I turned around, I seen
the lightning flashing down, and I knew
something had to give
if I was going to live
another day.

Fell down to my knees, and prayed
My God, my God, oh please
one more time
Get me through this night
show me the way.

Shook all day that night
as I was fearing for my life
then father came.
He lead me to safety
forever changed.

Striving not to sin
I want to fully let him in
and let him stay.
For this I always pray
I will not sway.

For this I always pray
I will not sway
I will not sway.

*Shane Soleta*

# Ready or Not

Come with me Lord
I need you
Come carry me away
Into the hidden valley
Where those like me are saved

Depression is my reason
for crying out to you.
My heart, I feel
is burning.
With thoughts not new to you

Shackled with impatience
Caught up in my mind
I've been there
and I know it
The fear of falling through

Every time I fail me
I am failing you
Living like a hermit
Don't know how to change it
Desire is my poet

Lust is taking over
Camouflaged as love
Want a woman's touch
Want to call it love
Love I do not want.

# Prodigal Son

Oh Lord, my God
My love and savior
I praise your name
Esteem and honor

You turned my evil
into faith
you taught me how
to fear your name

at the rim of hell
I stumbled with pride
You gave me a push
Then held me tight

I felt your hope
and made it my own
By your grace I was saved
You bought back my soul

By the blood of your son
Your free gift to all
I prayed for forgiveness
and answered your call

Thank you again lord
For all that you've done
And thanks from my mother
Who now has a son

*Shane Soleta*

# Lust

With my life
In God's hands
I need not fear
Yet still I am

Fearful of
Myself and I
My heart trembles
Within my mind

The demons which
I won't let go
The lusting flesh
Deprives my soul

Of knowing love
and all it is
From flying free
Away from sin

I ask you Lord
For mercy please
Cast out the lust
and fantasies

Let me see
and not undress
Make pure my heart
May I confess

I've thought wrong
and know this Lord
Even as
I loved your word

With your strength
I must believe
Through your son
You set me free.

*Shane Soleta*

# Waiting

Over and under
the way I am,
Waiting for you again.

Somehow I've got
to lose, to win,
Waiting for you again.

You caught me before
and I was scared
yet it seemed to feel right.

Thought I had enough
No way was I going back
I was in a special place.

The door slammed shut
but I took a peak.
Played naïve and fell asleep

My faith blew away
in the evil wind
Sometimes I just want to sin.

Hard to hold on
when you want to do wrong.
Seems that you must to fit in.

Do I shake the dice twice?
Do I walk away?
Do I continue to wait?

God please believe me
when I do pray.
Want it so bad to do right.

But I delight in the sin
of the evil winds
Desire betrays my eyes.

Need to slow down
Need to let go
Maybe I need to follow.

I was waiting for you
You were waiting for me
I needed to turn around.

I was running away
Pretending naïve
Wanted it my own way.

Help me believe
I want to believe
Am I waiting for you?
Are you waiting for me?

# The Plan

Friends in fold
My fellow man
Love of God
Live out the plan

The lonely road
Grabs my heart
What took so long
For life to start

I thank you God
And praise your name
Because of you
I'll be okay

This life of mine
Begin to live
Let go the past
Release my sins

I'll honor you
And do my best
On my heart
May you impress

This dream of yours
Just for me
May I be blessed
Accept these things

I want to help
My fellow man
My friends in fold
Reveal your plan.

*Shane Soleta*

# Holding on for Love

Holding
Whispering gray
of an autumn day.

Innocence
Reborn again
Through Jesus Christ.

All his love
pours down on me.
I'm just a seed
whose barely grown.

Searching for that place
so close to home.
So close is she
This love of mine
I want to know.

Where goes,
Learning all I can
before I am called home.
Don't want to be alone.
Father give me hope
do not close my eyes.

Allow,
Let my love arrive
Help me live alive
Take away the mind
that somehow wants to die.

These words I write, believe.
I pray you may be pleased.
I pray she soon may come.
I'm holding on for love.

*Shane Soleta*

# The Eagle

I turned my life – into nothing but madness
The sadness I felt – was the air that I breathed

I was waiting for dreams – to drop down from the sky
I thought the world – revolved around me

But I don't want to wish – on the stars that are falling
They are all dying – alone in the night

I want to be – the eagle who's flying
Who spreads his wings – and knows he is free

The sky is his love – the eagle is me
I surrender my will – and my selfish ways

The sky is his love – the eagle is me
The sky's never ending – as his love is for me

I've came to believe – the only thing stopping
My dreams and my love – the enemy me

I've learned to let go – and let God do my dreaming
I've turned it all over – and came to believe

I had to face death – and run like a child
Our father's arms – are open and free

The sky is his love – the eagle is me
I waited, I'm flying – his love sets me free

# Fighting

From into the night
This trembling heart
Is bursting with fear
Lost and alarmed

From out of the window
It all looks the same
But something is different
I have to change

Little by little
It won't work for me
I feel alone
Abandoned by thee

I had it all
And smoked it away
There is a chance
If I start today

More drastic the better
It's all I know
All or nothing
If I'm rich, I'm still broke

With a soul as demanding
And a mind full of shame
Lusting for something
In the past brought me pain

So how can it be
I want to be free
Yet I want reassurance
With a love just for me

The answer it lingers
My heart an abyss
From sins still committed
With knowledge of this

Still I am waiting
Still I'm alone
Lost in the shadows
Between faith and hope

Now how do I
Seek reconcile
My heart and my soul
With God reunite

Even as I say
I believe in you Lord
My mind finds away
To doubt and want more

I remember the time
When you gave me a taste
Of where I am headed
To your warm embrace

Still I do falter
The path which I choose
Psalm, one thirty-nine
Won't even do

I am unworthy
As ever or more
Beg you for mercy
My mind is a whore

Please God forgive me
In your son's name
Jesus please help me
And show me the way

How many chances
Must I request?
Before I find faith
Will I get it right yet?

My eyes you have saved
My feelings still gray
Please show me your will
and give me your strength

I alone know I'm helpless
I alone is in vain
Please Lord hold me close
and bring me no shame
I turn back the pages
and smoke the last one
The soldiers of evil
Cut off by the son

*Shane Soleta*

I spit out the demons
They circle and fade
Their laughter is gone
and so is my rage

I'm tired of fighting
I give it to God
Tired of writing
It's time to start living.

# Angels of Light

Lightning cross the river
Claims a wounded soul
Calling him to Heaven
Still I did not know

Sudden came the rain
Ozzfest in my ears
How many laughed out loud?
How many were in tears?

Inside I was drowning
Shot up out of hope
Medicated mind
How lost was my soul?

Lay next to the river
Angels far from sight
Right before my eyes
Brain dead I was blind

The night before they called
We called them northern lights
I now believe they were Angels
Angels of the light

Praise be to the Heavens
Who battled for my soul
Help me catch the falling
Before they too let go.

# If I

## Then anyone

If I
Then anyone

If I
Then anyone

Secrets kill.
Tell God and someone you trust your secrets
And the truth will set you free.

These poems still speak to me and I pray at least one of them has spoken to you. Thank you for reading them. That is all I could ever ask for. Most of the poems since I found God were written in my first year of recovery.

This book is about my personal journey here on Earth. I would hope that everyone who reads this has already found God or perhaps is now open to the possibility of there being a God. Whatever your higher power may be I wish you luck on your journey. The rest of this book will speak about my spiritual experiences and how friends have touched my life with their own poetry.

The following two poems are my favorites. They were written to me by one friend I met while I was in Woodstock and another one who I knew most of my life, but we really didn't become friends until she also found recovery and God while going to Woodstock. I keep the originals in my wallet and pull them out on days when I am struggling, to help me keep going or just to look back and reflect on where we came from. They always make me smile and sometimes a tear or two of joy trickles down. All three of us should be dead. We are so fortunate to have found God, he loves us so much. He wants us to be happy. I can truly say that I am today.

# Shane,

I can't find the words I need to say
For what you did for me that Saturday.

I feel so close now, it's all so true
Believing the Lord has worked through you

Life was getting tough, I couldn't bare
And like an angel you appeared there

Feeling so close to the man above
It is so true about unconditional love

My brother in faith is absolutely true
When out of town, I sure miss you

In the past you would come and go
Now our friendship only grows and grows

I think you're a very special man
So please keep in touch when you can

Cause this feeling of closeness isn't going away
I think of you Shane, faithfully everyday

New Life, the name couldn't be more true
God is looking out for the welfare of me and you

So I thank him daily for giving me a special friend
Thank God for you Shane it is the perfect end.

Your friend (sister) in Christ,
Gina

I can only look back
to that little room
where we met.
The fear in your eyes
was the feeling
in my heart.
Only did God know
this was your
chance, for a brand
new start.
I have watched you
cry.
I have felt your pain
I see your happiness
that will keep you sane
Take this new life
that God has in store.
And always remember
that drugs can't
hurt you
No more…

May God be with you always,

Tonya

*Shane Soleta*

# Journal entry

## 2 pm,
## 3/04/01

I just finished with my 2<sup>nd</sup> and 3<sup>rd</sup> step worksheet. I feel the presence of God in me like I never have before. I know you know what that feeling is. Thanks for believing in me. Praise be to God. The power of feeling at peace with myself is awesome. Thank you, thank you, thank you.

I feel so full of him right now, dare I say I almost feel like a chosen one, which I have felt before, but ran from that feeling because it scared me to feel that good about myself. But I think it is o.k. to feel that way as long as I don't go around telling everyone how special I am. And I truly believe everyone is chosen and they just need to allow themselves to be filled with his love, but all I can do to show them is to live by example and continue my journey back home, by showing love to everyone. I think I'm o.k. with that. Thanks, you are truly an Angel on earth. I love you as I love everyone. Praise God.

I really want to talk to you, so please don't test my patience too long on Monday. I'm not trying to say you have tested me in the past. I'm just usually the last one. O.k. I'll shut up and I will be patient. Just don't push it too far. Ha ha, o.k. I'll calm down. Talk to you later, bet you forgot my book. I've never felt so in tune before. Since I was a child anyway.

2:55 pm,
3/04/01

I'm wandering around floating like I'm on the best drug
I've ever felt. I hope I don't come down hard. It is
unbelievable the way I feel. There are so many people here
and I feel just overwhelmed by all the love this place is full
of. I'm sitting in the group room and I'm breathing very
heavy.

I've been introduced to some people, but I don't remember
hardly any names. I feel completely lost, like I'm in another
world. I'm feeling emotions too deep and too real for words
to describe, it's almost like I'm outside of my body, no, I
am outside of my body and uneasy, yet so at peace.
No drug in the world can do this, because I really am not
afraid to come down. This dimension has always been here
and either I was afraid, blind, or it just didn't matter. I'm
going to meditate and start work on my 2$^{nd}$ step. Wow!

End of journal entry

Those were the exact words I used to describe my
spiritual awakening. They don't even come close. I entered
treatment not believing in God, I thought the Feds were
watching me and trying to kill me. I was a basket case,
scared of everyone and everything. I had not used in two
days and still the paranoia would not go away.

I silently said to whoever was listening, "o.k. God, if you
exist, you better show yourself to me and you better
actually be there or I am going to die."

It was something to that effect anyway. I needed a God
or I would die. That was very clear to me. Somewhere in

those first couple of days I prayed to the one I had disowned for too many years. I had been there about twelve days when my awakening took place. I had accepted God and found some peace in my life. The paranoia was still there, but not nearly as bad as that first day.

There was a question on that worksheet asking what I would do if I found out I had a terminal disease and had only one year to live. This is something my various using friends and I had mulled over several times throughout the years. My answer then was, quit my job, party my butt off, and take out a few cops I hated. That is putting it lightly anyway.

Like I said before, at this time I had accepted God and for the most part I now felt pretty safe. The way I answered the question still surprises me. I think God was directing me.

"I would work six months, if possible, and save as much money as I could. Then I would start hitchhiking west and whoever it was that picked me up, I would tell them about God and what he had done for me." That could not possibly have come from me at that point in time, but I remember writing it as vividly today as I did back then.

The second I finished writing it, it happened. A wave of something filled me up from the bottom of my feet to the top of my head. I knew what it was, yet I had never felt anything like it before in my life. I believe it was a taste of what is to come. I remember being in shock for awhile, because nothing on this Earth feels that good, nothing!

I felt as if I belonged to and was a part of everything. I left the room I was working in and started walking around the treatment center. I could not feel my legs and it actually did feel like I was floating down the halls. There was a voice inside of me that I just knew came from God, and it

110

was telling me. "We are all connected. We all come from God and are all trying to get back to him. We are all in this together." I could not wipe the smile off my face at everyone I saw that day. Everything seemed a thousand times more vivid and beautiful than anything. The sky, the air I breathed, all the different people there visiting, the trees outside. It was a completely different world than the one I had lived in my entire life. A million times more intense than any drug I had ever experienced and yet I had never felt so at peace and so loved. It was God, it was Love, and yes, God Is Love!

That whole experience lasted around three hours. I completed both my 2$^{nd}$ and 3$^{rd}$ written steps while feeling the awakening. I truly believe it was the Holy Spirit at work in me that day. I have had similar experiences since then. One was just two days later while reading my recovery bible. None of them have come close to the intensity of the first one, but each one is special and unique and filled with love.

Some have told me it is not wise to tell people about your spiritual experiences. They won't understand and may think you are crazy. I wouldn't blame anyone for thinking I am crazy. I have become the person I used to hate. I'm a Christian who believes Jesus Christ gave his life on the cross for my sins. I try to live my life in a way that would please God.

This is not the person I wanted to be when I grew up. I am crazy, crazy in love with Jesus and crazy because I go to as many 12 step meetings as I can. All my life I felt different, I just didn't fit in and I looked at the world with a set of eyes unlike those anyone else possessed. I seemed to experience greater joys and became sick with deeper pains.

My emotions were a tangled mess and in constant battle with each other.

The only way I could ever feel at ease was with some sort of chemical in my body. The only place I seemed to fit in was with other people who also used drugs. It was easy to get accepted, just show up with drugs or money to get them and you were in.

I've been told that as recovering people we have two choices. Keep coming to meetings and hanging around other recovering addicts or else go back and hang out with people who are using and start using again. Do you want to live or do you want to die?

1/08/03

# In Here

I owe you my life
I'm afraid to give it to you
You never left my side
But I don't trust you
Why would you trust me?

I've praised you and loved your word
Cursed, abused, and betrayed you
I have loved you like a child
Hated you like a man
Refused to fear you

Yet here I stand
I have given you everything
Taken it all back
And given it to you again
Called you my best friend

I surrendered
Raised the white flag
Just to ambush and run
Still you love
Still you love

I cannot understand
Why it is I'm still alive
So many better have died
Your son was crucified

*Shane Soleta*

## Still I am alive

So many gifts you've given
Yet I refuse to open
My passions are not hidden
Yet I'm so scared to fail
Feeling I am broken
Of your name I've been ashamed
So tell me why you love me
I will never understand
Through triumph and through pain
You love me anyway.

# About the Author:

Shane Soleta always wanted to know why. Why do people hurt eachother intentionally? Why do people cheat on their spouses, beat their children, get divorced, abandon the ones they are supposed to love, why do we take so much pleasure in watching someone else's pain?

Shane started writing lyrics for songs in the 6th grade. Once he reached 11th grade he was writing them on a daily basis. Many of these were ballads of impending death and suicidal fantasies. Others were sexually charged, rock n' roll stories he intended to live. He wanted to be a rock idol and party all the time. He never lacked the desire to have a good time no matter what the cost.

He graduated from Windom Area High School in 1987. His plans were to go to vocational school for audio technology, find a band to sing one of his songs, sell a million records, retire and party the rest of his life. If not a song, he would write a book and do the same thing. He really believed this.

Lacking the self-discipline to learn the guitar and being preoccupied with living the rock life style his writing turned more towards poetry. He dropped out of vocational school and a little over a year later found himself in jail for selling marijuana.

Nine months after his release from jail Shane was in college. He lived with friends who appreciated his poetry and his partying ways. He started selling drugs again and writing more and more poetry. He used to curse God for giviing him a talent he felt would be useless in making a living at. How do you get rich writing poems?

The drugs he was inhaling on a daily basis seemed to help his creativity. They gave him different ways to experience and express the self-hatred and pain he always felt, and was very good at hiding from others. He also believed that all great writers were alcoholics and drug addicts. Therefore he was only doing what he was supposed to do to become a great writer.

His days at Mankato State were some of the best and worst days of his life. A creative writing class changed his idea of what poetry should be. Many of the poems in the book are from 1991 to 1994. He dropped out of college in 1992 and moved to Colorado.

There he was introduced to meth and his life would never be the same. He recalls seeing demons flying around his bedroom that first night he used. He was unable to sleep and thought it was the coolest thing he had ever experienced. Having lived in Grand Junction 3 months before this happened, just 3 months later he was moving home to Minnesota to get away from it.

It wasn't long before meth was everywhere in Minnesota as well. When he stopped believing in God completely in 1994 he had been back home for nearly a year and a half. That was the last year he ever loved anyone and when his poetry virtually stopped. He wrote very little over the next six years. The drugs that used to help his writing now did not allow him to write. He had lost his soul and the desire to live and love. He knew he was already killing himself so the idea of suicide he never considered very strongly, as that would happen on its own at any time. Many of his friends had went that way and his ego reallized how soon they were forgotten.

Finally, after trying to quit on his own, having a bad trip from shooting up meth, and almost killing himself he put himself in treatment. There he found God and his writing took off in ways that he never could have imagined. God had given him his gift back and he began writing for others as well as himself. The freedom that comes from surrendering to God is the main focus. Also the ability to be honest about what he is feeling and to be honest with God even when he is depressed or feeling lonely. Being human these feelings are real and valid, Shane believes by telling God what he feels, God is then able to release him from that burden. If he is truly willing to let them go.

Shane continues going to 12 step meetings and pursuing a closer relationship with his savior, Jesus Christ. He currently works for a directional drilling company and recently earned his real estate appraiser's license. He contiues to write poetry and lyrics and wants to write his complete story when the time is right. He feels it is still too soon to write his full story. Til that day comes we can weep for his past and celebrate his future through his poetry and words of encouragement in this book. I wish him all the best in his recovery and the search of a better life through God and his 12 step meetings.

Printed in the United States
1125100001B/403-426